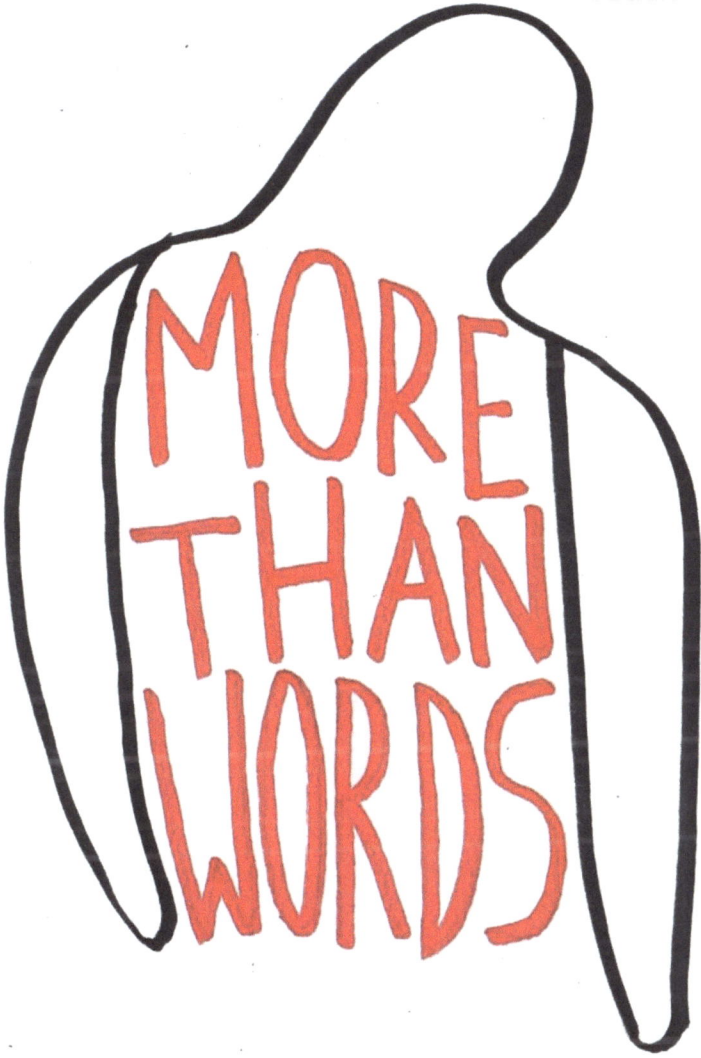

VERNON LOGAN

MORE THAN WORDS

by V. V. Logan

Artwork by YoYo Ferro

Dedicated to those that live life to the fullest and inspire others to do the same.

Published by

www.ebooksolutions.org

For book author appearance inquiries and interviews contact the Author at

info@loganventures.com

ISBN-13:
978-0692264119

ISBN-10:
0692264116

Table of Contents

REFLECTION OF A VICTIM 6

CHAINED 8

HYPERNATREMIA 10

(UNTITLED) 12

A MOTHER'S LOVE 14

HOLY TRINITY 16

NO PLACE LIKE HOME 18

CLOUDS 20

FINISHED PRODUCT 22

OBSESSION 24

MUST BE MAGIC 26

OPEN 28

WOUNDED 30

CONSTANT CONTACT 32

CARRYING ON 34

BLIND MAN 36

RESPONSIBLE 38

MORE THAN WORDS 40

CRAZY 42

IN THE RAIN 44

REFLECTION OF A VICTIM

I think it prowler. Like Jack the Ripper.
Stalking it's victims, leaving them
Mortally wounded,
In stealth,
Unidentifiable and leaving no trace.
Love is a fucking villain.

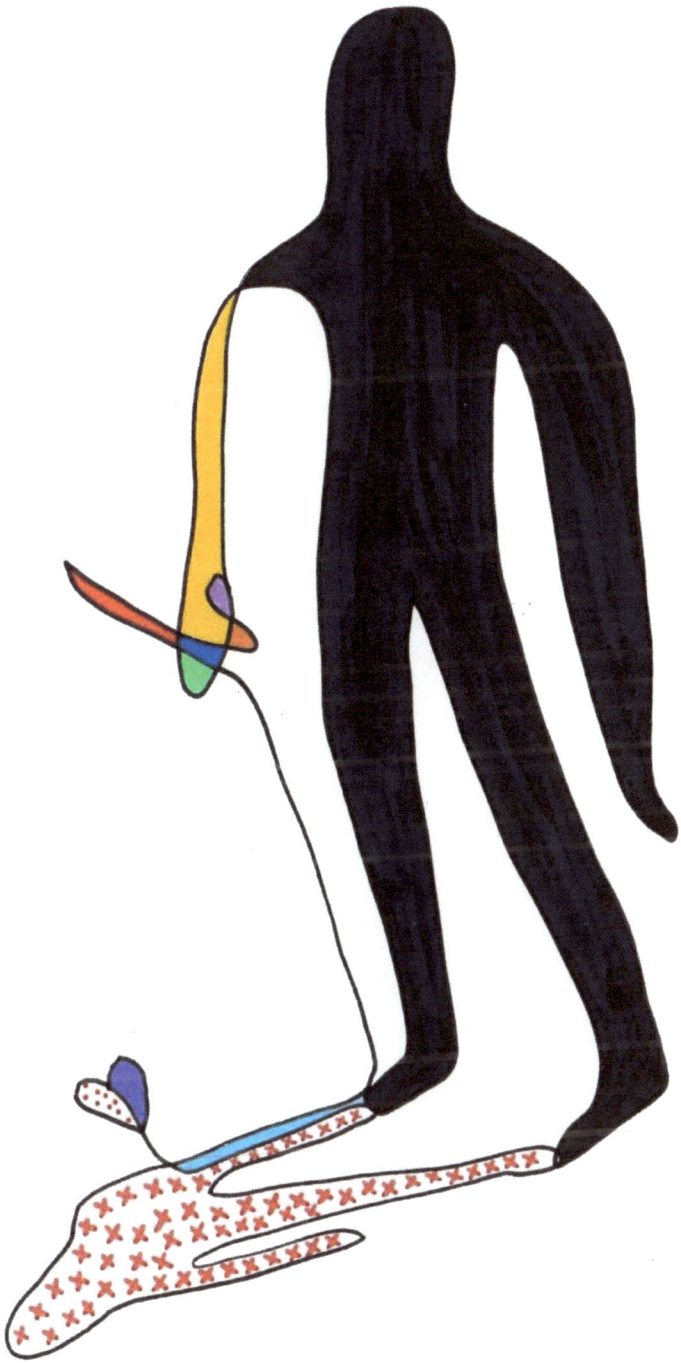

CHAINED

Some loves are never to be spoken.
Often never to bloom.
Hidden in passing.
Chained by circumstance.
Buried deep within our souls.
Confined to elevators, quick glances, and temporary stares.
More than words.
We remain chained.

HYPERNATREMIA

Constantly thirsting, spirit bound.
My pitcher running over with love and I'm dying to take a sip.
Thousands of miles away.
Still feeling delusional and begging to be poured more.
Anxious and unruly, salivating but I can figure out how to
quench this unending thirst.

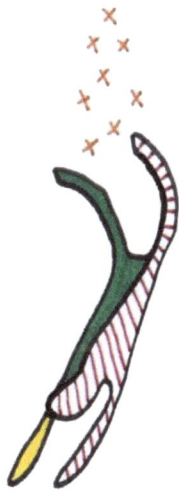

(UNTITLED)

Honesty and truth of love is not truth and honesty of love to all.

A MOTHER'S LOVE

So natural to some and so foreign to so many.
Part of character or chemistry, DNA and maybe destiny.
Unequalled and unexplainable.
Unbelievable and irreplaceable.
Like a fabric woven throughout time.
Fine and gentle, strong and pure.

HOLY TRINITY

On a journey of awakening.
Love at the

forefront,

leading the

way. Often

discovered

in the oddest

places.

My soul the only available translator.
Illusive by nature incomprehensible.
Determined to understand their ways.
Life, love and beauty worshiped.
Searching for the temple, somewhere to hear the good news.
The gospel lay in them and is them.
 They became the new holy trinity.

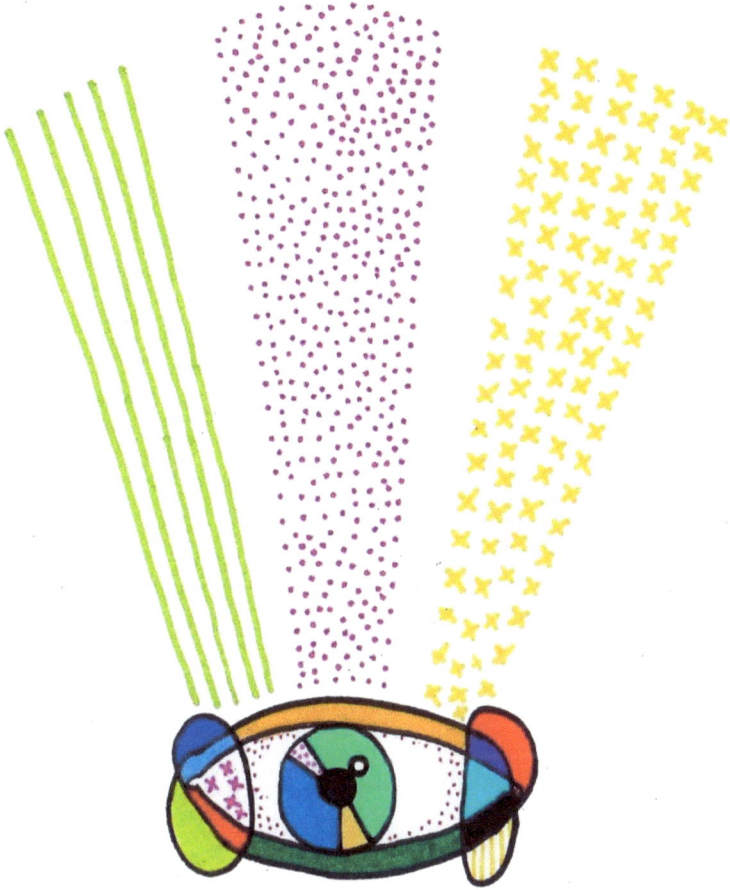

NO PLACE LIKE HOME

There's no place like home.
The history, the memories and all the possibilities.
Made real by all that made me.
The names, the places and faces.
Lives lived and lives lost.
All the sacrifices and celebrations.
Done without one thought of who and what I might be.
At one time called the future.
Now I wonder about what might be my legacy.

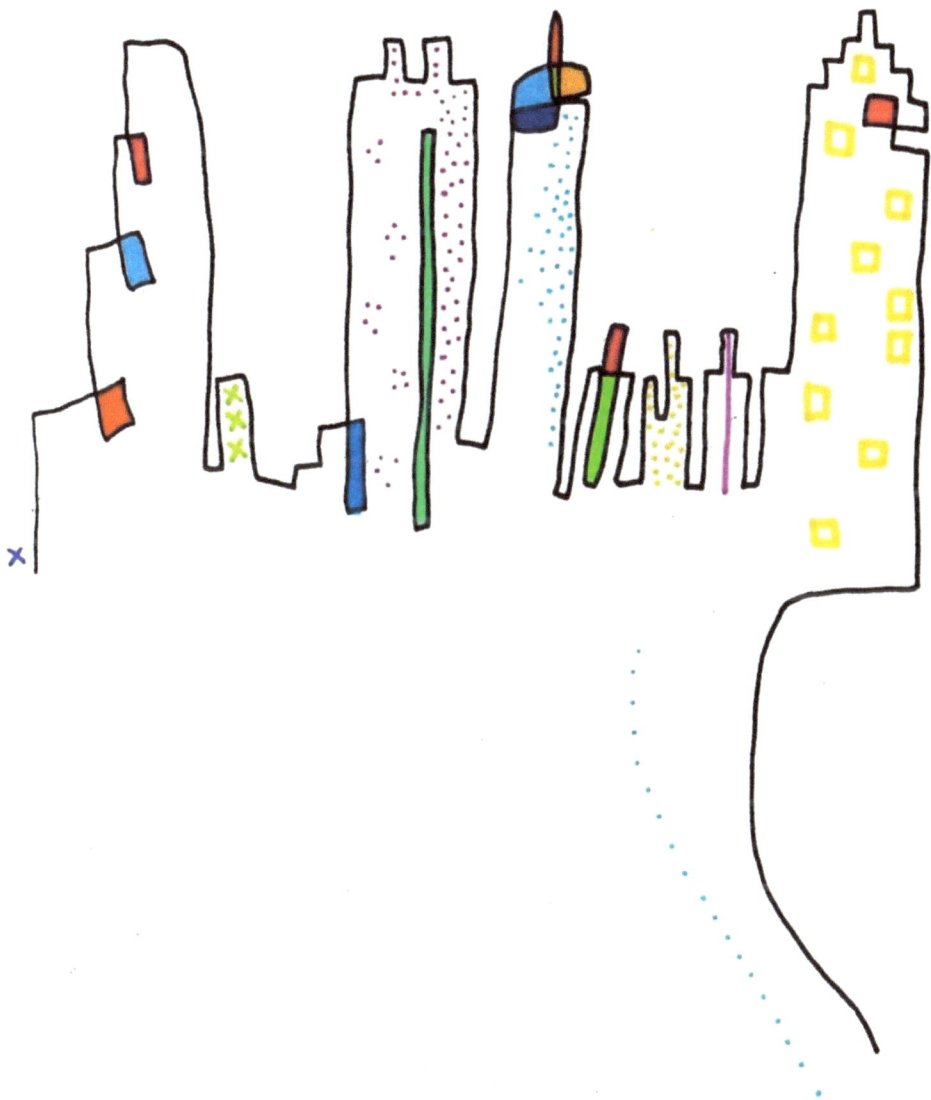

CLOUDS

It can blur your vision.
Cloud and distort as it consumes you.
An entrancing siren in the mist.
Hiding in the wilderness like a sly beast calling itself
inspiration.
Bowing before nothing and no man.
Glorious and renewing like a sunrise and refreshing like a
summer breeze.
Draining like the desert.
More like clouds blocking the but never raining down
rejuvenation.

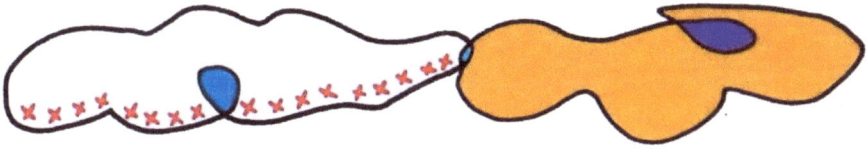

FINISHED PRODUCT

Clearly all the stops, detours, roadblocks and potholes have a purpose.
At the end there should be a finished product.
From raw materials forged.
Refined and polished.
Shaped and molded, massaged and formed.
Pounded, filing and grinding day in and day out.
The tears poured out and blood spilled.
All I've done to find the finished product of me.

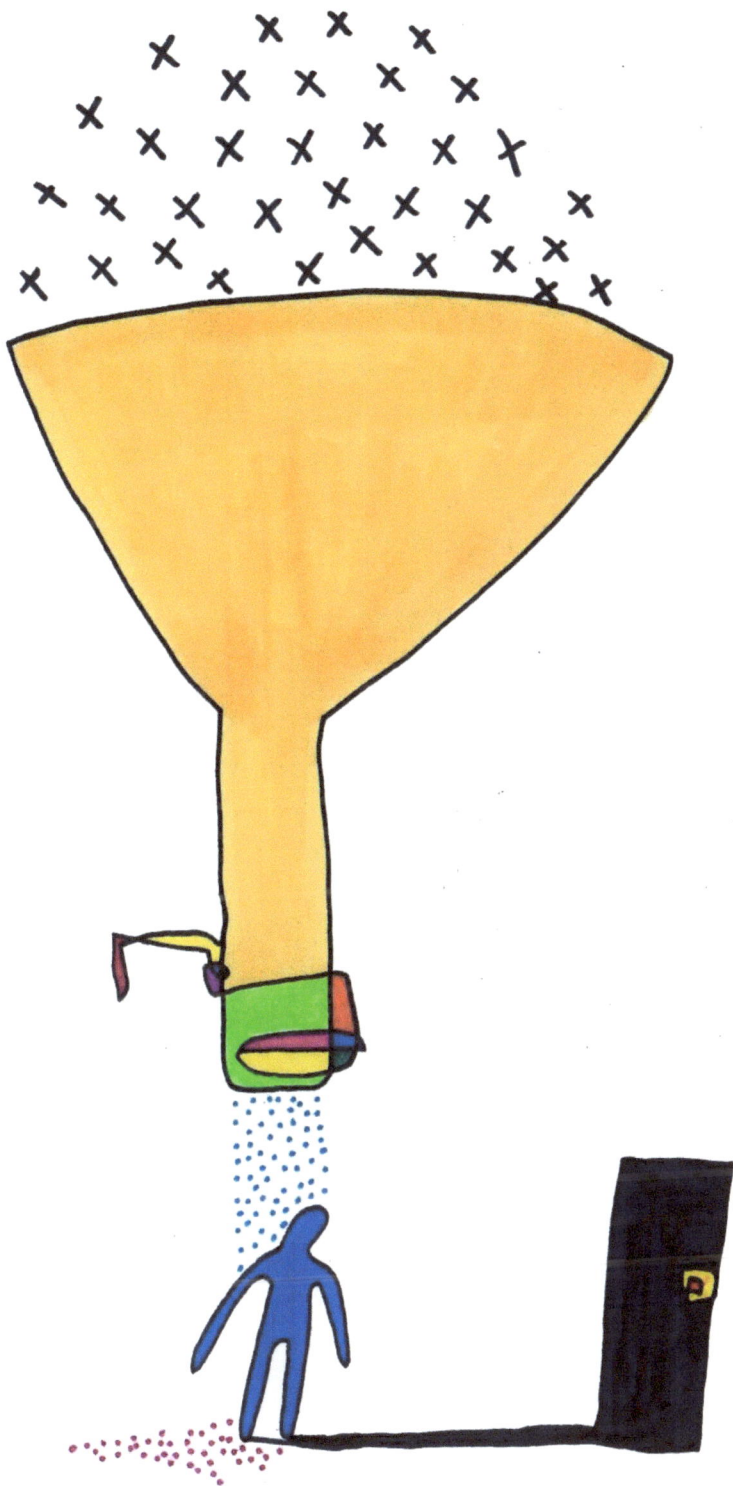

OBSESSION

Caught up in the conversation.
A friend, a lover, that special someone you want to go on and
on.
Be it written, you're reading without ceasing.
Over and over again looking and searching.
Wanting to find some deeper meaning or where they might be
trying to say just a little more.
That understanding you might have missed the first few
times.
Chatting, the typing getting faster over miles of the
information highway.
Over the phone where you want them to get just a little closer
to the receiver.
Occasionally, so crystal clear you almost feel their breath on
your face.
Each new topic seemingly more magical than the last.
The sound and inflection never getting old.
Over meals, a glass of wine, a stiff drink, coffee.
Maybe even the fog of tobacco or some other herbal essence.
All mad a little bit better because of your obsession.

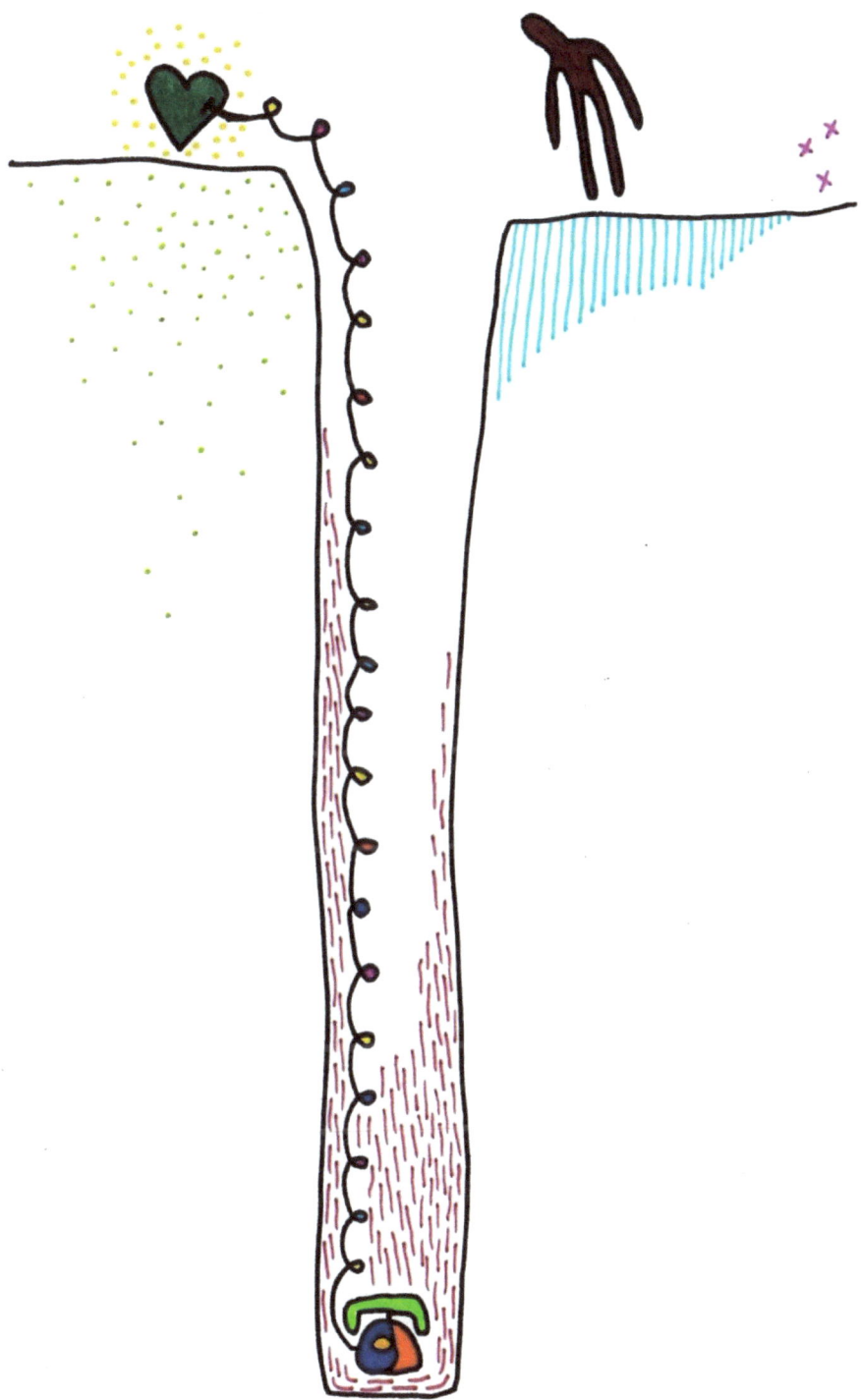

MUST BE MAGIC

This shit is hard.
Definitely more difficult than calculus or chemistry.
But physics the shit ain't.
More like magic.
The words might sound simple, but hell it's hard to get them out.
The execution and pronunciation hardly if ever come out just right.
Biggest thing is that you just have to damn well believe,
because it must be magic.
Part love.
Part convenience.
Part luck.
Part pleasure.
Part passion.
Potion divine.

OPEN

Often wondered why I've been so open.
Always known it would be to the detriment of me.
Always known who I was and what I wanted to be.
Been so bottled up trying to keep the heartache from getting at me.
Never had a desire to be free from all the yearning within me.
Never had the chance to take a stance and force myself just to let go freely.
Pried open and left unsealed vulnerable to the world.
Open to be seen and open to be felt.
Open to the dangers anew, snuck up on me and left me open before I knew it, my soul was drained dry.

WOUNDED

Calling for the medic.
Screaming out for help.
Jumping from plane to plane.
Running like Forest.
Drowning in drinks.
Driving as fast as I could.
Filled up with food so I almost faint.
I couldn't even hear myself think.
They couldn't save me.
So instead I started breathing into me and pumping on my
chest to revive myself.
Working on me.

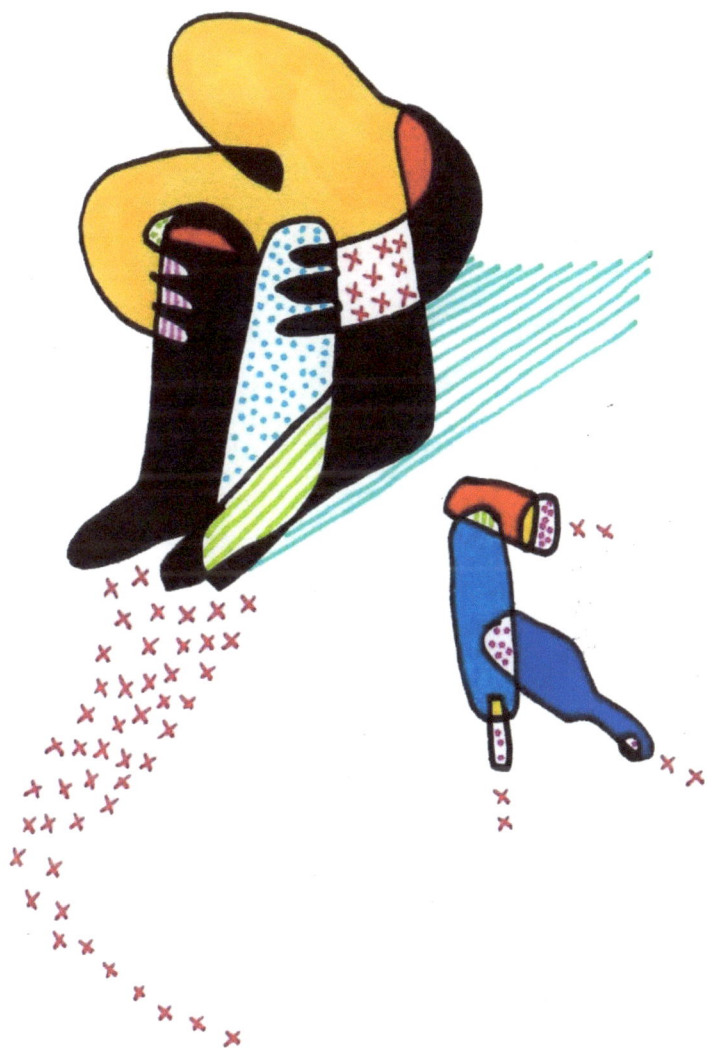

CONSTANT CONTACT

Sometimes in life people cross paths.
Wanting and looking for something different and completely different.
Often passing like two planets in orbit.
Never touching, only seeing each other once and only briefly aligned ever so infrequently.
Other times like the moon and celestial projectiles.
In constant contact, colliding forever on a collision course with each other.

CARRYING ON

The cocktails, the garnish, and all the chasers were gone.
All the wine has been poured.
What we were left with were each other.
Company departed, all the amenities were off.
Each inch of the table cleared and whipped down.
Thoughts and intentions clear.
Ecstasy in our eyes and fantasies abound.
Scents of jasmine or vanilla lingered.
Sounds of Ibrahim played as we continued to carry on.
We didn't mind that the lights stayed on.

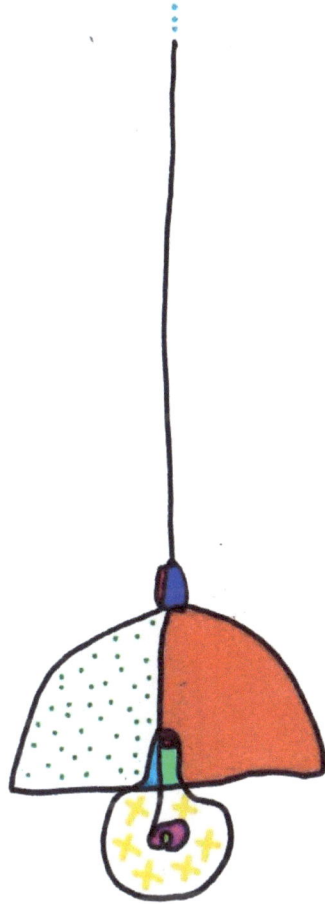

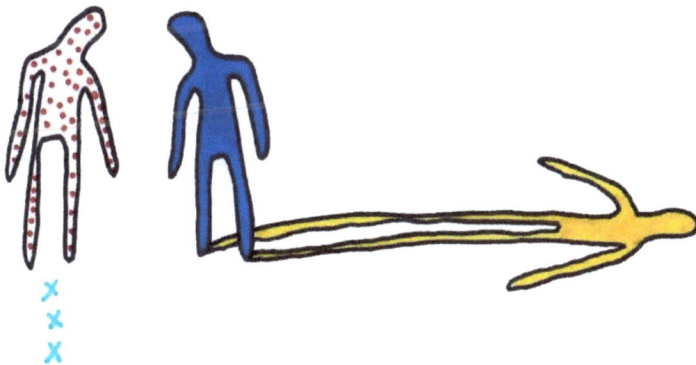

BLIND MAN

A blind man wouldn't be the wiser.
Especially if he had never seen a thing.
He no longer waited on the sun to rise to start living.
No care for when it sets.
Never once asked to have his sight restored.
Now days pass swiftly and every minute is consumed.
He doesn't linger anywhere.
He won't even give people the time to stare.
Moving forward with no regrets.
Living for today and not tomorrow.
Never letting the fear of not knowing stop him from growing.
Staying wiser was a way of life I learned from the blind man.

RESPONSIBLE

Overwhelming feeling.
A sense of responsibility for someone.
An attachment not easily let go, the immense pleasure of it all.
The power that it brings, the joy of making someone happy.
The smile on their face.
The food on their plate, the clothes you would give them off your back.
It's all part of the responsibility.
Daring to do what needs to be done.
What's right or what's wrong as long as it's in their favor.
Blurring the lines and crossing others.
Creating new lanes creating traffic and tragedy with no worries.
All worth it when you're responsible for another.

MORE THAN WORDS

Some seek to sample this delicacy.
Futile attempts to fish, trap or track this beast.
It devours hunters as its prey.
It lurks in the cities, it lurks in the hills, drinks in nearby streams.
Looming in the desert.
Sleeping neither day nor night.
No one seeks it for prize or sport.
But for peace and satisfaction.
Seeking the comfort and warmth it provides might just be worth it if you survive.
But you will need more than words.

CRAZY

Like a mad man, nothing new to me.
Torn and confused, full of new ideas.
Rushing to seek patience.
Frantic over trying to be calm.
Dodging danger with hopes of being able to lay dormant.
Begging for which is already mine.
Eating when I should seek out a drink.
Sleeping and dying for the opportunity.
Loving the taste of life's poisonous and strange fruit.
Blessings recklessly set free.
Given so easily and taken advantage right before me.
Neglected myself wanting to be mistreated by some.
Decisions you can't take back refreshed in that fact.
Pleased to be out of control of closed chapters, crazy when it is
all said and there is nothing to be done.

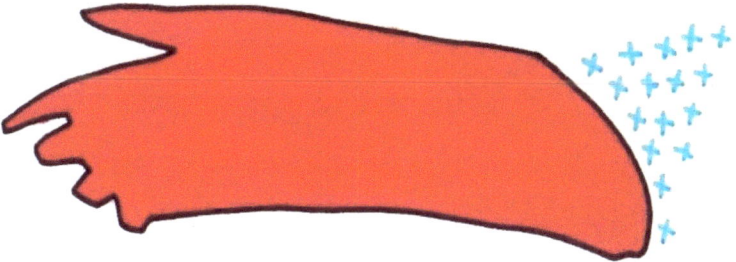

IN THE RAIN

He stood there in the rain begging and pleading on the phone
like a fool.
Command, ask, request, even suggest for him to make the
move.
All he wanted was a reason.
It didn't matter the season.
To offer up himself as that human sacrifice.
The time and place was of no consequence.
He wanted to be planted near her, cutting off a chuck of self.
Willing to uproot it all.
Wanting to change and redirect, no reason to speculate.
Drenched in sadness not one tear fell.
For years he would wait patiently.
Convinced she was the one.
Still standing in the rain he had failed.

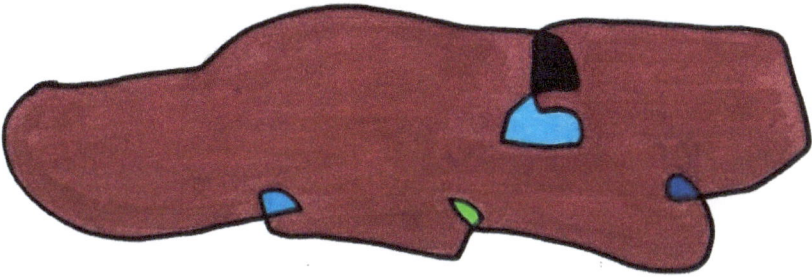

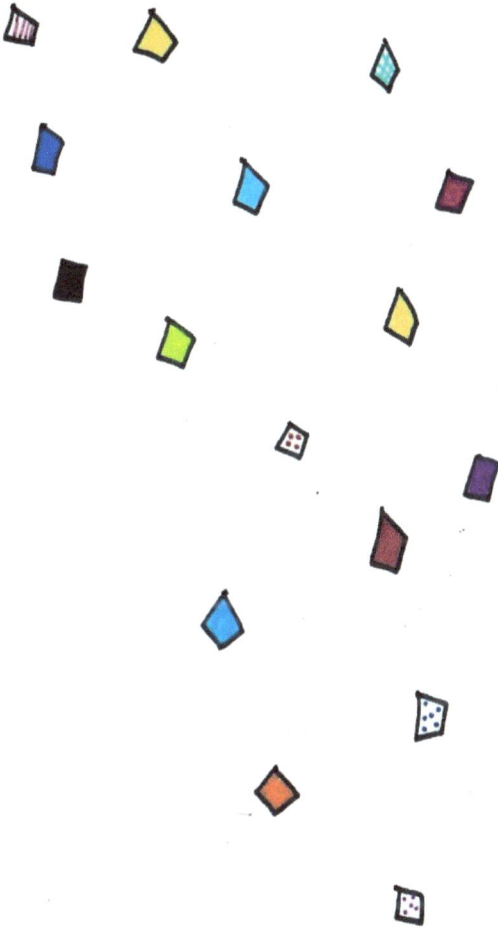

THE END

Vernon is an American accomplished poet, journalist and researcher based in Atlanta, GA. His works are focused on analysis delivered in metaphor and prose. He is inspired by all aspects of the human experience. The motto Eat.Drink.Live is his approach to life. His current projects include pre-production for producing a series of short films based on the exploration of the human experience as well as a qualitative research study based on market penetration utilizing social media.

For further information about Vernon Logan, please check:

velogan

vesinister

morethanwords

morethenwords563@gmail.com

Yoyo Ferro is a Brazilian artist based in Atlanta, GA. His artworks are marked by a mix of pop art, blind contour animals, cityscapes and origami. Yoyo's love for Atlanta, since his moving to the city in 2010, has inspired him to document the city skyline in many of his works. An origami enthusiast, Yoyo has a parallel project, the "Yoyo Ferro 1000 Origami Cranes", where he mails origami cranes to people around the world with the intention to incentive connection and creativity.

For further information about Yoyo, please check:

📷 yoyoferro

🐦 yoyoferro

f facebook.com/yoyoferro

✉ yoyoferro@live.com

www.ingramcontent.com/pod-product-compliance
Lightning Source LLC
Chambersburg PA
CBHW041358090426
42739CB00005B/55